AF454634

Sing for Me Sarah

"This book is dedicated to the future generations of children who have the courage to step into the spotlight. Ilse, Edmund and Jonah, may you find your own voice where ever life takes you." - Carol Selick

Find More Children's Books & Music at: www.CarolSelickBooks.com

www.SlothDreamsBooks.com

Copyright ©2024 by Carol Selick
Copyright ©2024 for Illustrations & Cover Design by KeriAnne N. Jelinek

All rights reserved, including the right of reproduction in whole are in part in any form. Sloth Dreams Books & Publishing, LLC. and colophon are registered trademarks of Sloth Dreams Books & Publishing, LLC.

Published by Sloth Dreams Books & Publishing, LLC.
Sloth Dreams Children's Books
Pennsylvania, USA
www.SlothDreamsBooks.com

All Rights Reserved.

ISBN: 978-2-4538-6601-3

Sing for Me, Sarah

Written by
Carol Selick

Illustrated by
KeriAnne Jelinek

TALENT
SHOW

FRIDAY,
May
21st

Sarah saw a sign in the school hallway.
TALENT SHOW FRIDAY, MAY 21ST

"Who wants to be in the talent show?" asked her teacher.

"Please write your name and special talent on this Sign-up Sheet."
Name:
Special Talent:
Alice
Piano
Chloe & Bella
Piano
Alex
Piano
Abby, Fiona, Shirley
Dance
Henry
Magician
BE THE CHANGE that you wish to SEE IN THE WORLD
You can do it!

Sarah
counted...

3 Dancers

4 Piano Players

5 Singers and...
1 Magician

She knew what her special talent was. Sarah loved to sing!

She sang with the birds outside her bedroom window.

Sarah sang on afternoon walks with her dog Coco.

She sang when her brother practiced his electric guitar.

Sarah dreamed of standing center stage with colored lights shining right on her.

Music was everywhere!
Mom listened to country music.

Dad played jazzy songs
in the car.

Sarah rushed home from school to tell her mother about the show.

"What song will you sing?"

Sarah froze.

Sarah opened her mouth to sing but no sound came out.

She took a deep breath and tried again.

"I can't sing!" she cried.

"Saltwater should help. Swish it around your mouth," Mom said.

"Ooh!" Sarah made a sour lemon face.

She tried again, but she still couldn't sing!

"How about some warm milk with honey?"

"That tastes better. I bet I can sing, now!"

But instead of La, La, La, she sounded like Ugh, Ugh, Ugh.

Sarah ran to her room and plopped down on the bed.

Then, she heard a sound that startled her.

It was a woman's voice singing higher and higher.

"Who's that?" Sarah asked her mother.

"It must be our new neighbor. I think she's an opera singer."

"Maybe she can help me," Sarah whispered.

"Good idea! I'll bring her a plate of raspberry cookies."

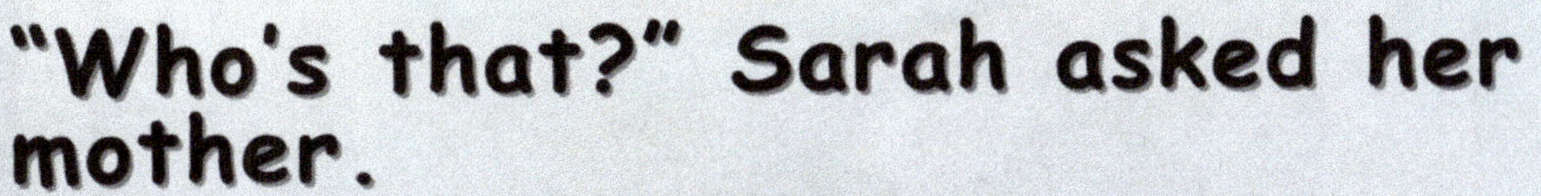

"Welcome to the neighborhood!"

"How lovely! So nice to meet you.
I am Miss Lorenzo. Please come in."

"We heard your beautiful voice
through our window. Are you an
opera singer?" asked Mom.

La Scala Opera House
Sydney Opera House
Frankfurt Opera House
"Yes!" Miss Lorenzo answered in a loud, booming voice.

Her bracelets made a jingling noise as she pointed to the posters on the wall.

"These are some of the places I've performed."

La Scala Opera House
Frankfurt Opera House
Covent Garden Opera House
"My daughter Sarah loves to sing, but she's lost her voice. Can you help her?"

"I can try. Open your mouth and say aaah, Sarah."
"Everything sounds normal. When did this happen?"
"Today, when I was choosing a song for the talent show."

"What kind of songs do you like?"

"I like country, jazzy songs, and rock songs. But I don't know what the whole school wants to hear!"

"I had a favorite song when I was your age. Can I play it for you?"

Miss Lorenzo's voice filled the room.

"I love it! Can I sing it for
the Talent Show?"

"Yes, sing it with me Sarah. If you
love the song, the audience will!"

Music, music everywhere. Sounds so different. I don't care. I can sing it my own way. Rock, jazz, country, let it play! Let me sing my song for you. Singing's what I love to do.

"I got my voice back!"

"Bellissima!"

Sarah practiced her song every day.
When they called her name the day
of the Talent Show, she was ready!

She walked onstage and felt the
warmth of the spotlight shining on
her. Her dream was coming true!
She sang:

Let me sing my song for you. Singing's what I love to do. I feel happy. I feel free. When I'm sounding just like me.

Music, music everywhere. Fast
songs, slow songs all to share.
Words and tunes to make my own.
Slide it, glide it, bring it home.

The audience clapped and Sarah took a bow. Then she heard a familiar voice.

"Bellissima!" It was Miss Lorenzo!

Carol Selick

Carol Selick is a music educator with a degree in Early Childhood and Elementary Education from Rutgers University.

Carol is a performing singer and songwriter. Her recordings, "Life is Believing in You" and "Just Gonna Think About Today", feature a mix of standards and originals.

She is the author of an award-winning coming-of-age book, "Beyond the Song" which is based on her early years in the music business. Carol also published a picture book – "Play for Me, Peter" which encourages children to learn to play the piano.

To find out more about Carol, please go to her website –

www.CarolSelickBooks.com

Music, Music Everywhere

Carol Selick

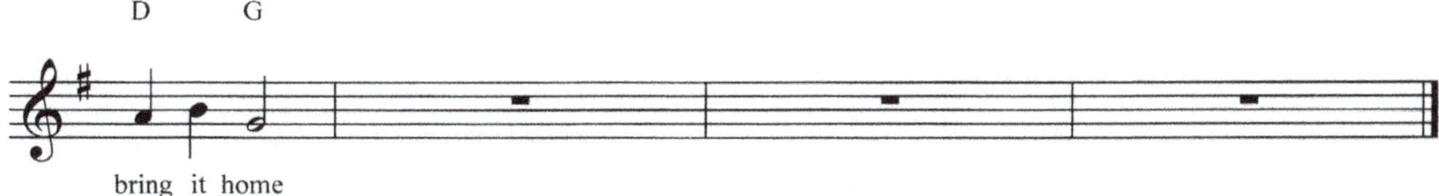

Sing for Me,
Sarah

www.ingramcontent.com/pod-product-compliance
Lightning Source LLC
LaVergne TN
LVHW080851240726
843527LV00052B/305